Counting on Faith

Written by
Maurice Prater

Illustrated by
Jason Koltuniak

Foreword by
Timothy Michael Cardinal Dolan

Divine Providence Press

Library of Congress Page

Published by Divine Providence Press
University of Mary
Catholic Studies Program
c/o Dr. Joshua Hren, Ph.D.
7500 University Drive
Bismarck, ND 58504

Divine Providence Press is an imprint of Wiseblood Books.
www.wisebloodbooks.com

To order, call (800) 288-6279 and ask for Dr. Joshua Hren, Ph.D.
www.divineprovidencepress.com

Library of Congress Cataloging-in-Publication Data

Counting on Faith / Maurice Prater

1.   Prater, Maurice, 1962-

2.   Children's Book

3.   Scriptural Counting Book

ISBN-13: 978-0692234334
ISBN-10: 0692234330

Scripture references are taken from *The Holy Bible: Douay-Rheims Version.*

Divine Providence Press works to spread the fragrance of Christ throughout the world, scattering little petals of providence by means of spiritual classics, devotional literature, children's books, and other writings that incarnate God's beauty and the splendor of truth.

Printed in the United States of America
First Edition

Foreword

Office of the Cardinal
1011 First Avenue
New York, NY 10022

When I was little, my teachers at Holy Infant School in Ballwin, Missouri, used to tell us stories from the Bible, and taught us to read the Bible. It was my favorite class!

It's the greatest Book ever, because God helped the writers tell us about Him, and how He wants us to live.

That's why I like this new little book, *Counting on Faith*, so much.

It helps us learn about God and our religion in an easy way, by going through so many numbers in the Bible.

God wants us to do *three* things:

1. To know Him

2. To love Him

3. To serve Him

This book helps us to do that!

Timothy Michael Cardinal Dolan
Archbishop of New York

January 24, 2014

AD QUEM IBIMUS

Can you count to 10?
Let's give it a try!

Number 1

We have one God,
and He is Our Father.

God the Father   1

Number 2

Long ago, God sent a great flood upon the earth.
He asked Noah to build an Ark and to take with him a pair of each animal.
A pair means two.

1 Male Animal + 1 Female Animal = 2 of Each Animal

Number 3

Jesus Christ is the Divine Son of God, and He grew up in a family of three people known as the Holy Family.

Jesus Christ	1
Blessed Virgin Mary	2
Saint Joseph	3

Number 4

The Holy Spirit wrote the Bible. In it, He wrote four books or Gospels about Jesus through four different human authors.

The Gospel According to Matthew	1
The Gospel According to Mark	2
The Gospel According to Luke	3
The Gospel According to John	4

St. Matthew

St. Mark

St. Luke

St. John

Number 5

Jesus died for our sins.
When He rose from the dead,
He showed His five wounds
to Saint Thomas the Apostle.
These wounds remained as marks
of salvation for all believers.

Right Hand	1
Left Hand	2
Right Foot	3
Left Foot	4
Right Side	5

Number 6

God created the world in six days.

Day 1	Day and Night
Day 2	Sky
Day 3	Earth
Day 4	Sun, Moon, and Stars
Day 5	Fish and Birds
Day 6	Animals and Humans

Day 1

Day 2

Day 3

Day 4

Day 5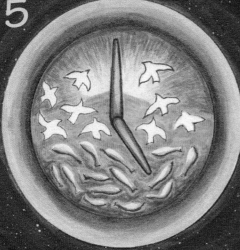

Day 6

Number 7

The seven gifts of the
Holy Spirit help us
to do what is *good*
in the eyes of God.

Gift 1	Wisdom
Gift 2	Understanding
Gift 3	Counsel
Gift 4	Fortitude
Gift 5	Knowledge
Gift 6	Piety
Gift 7	Holy Fear of the Lord

Number 8

In the *Our Father* prayer,
we ask God to help us eight times.

Our Father, who art in Heaven,	1
Hallowed be Thy Name.	2
Thy Kingdom come,	3
Thy Will be done, on earth as it is in Heaven.	4
Give us this day our daily bread,	5
And forgive us our trespasses,	
as we forgive those who trespass against us;	6
And lead us not into temptation,	7
But deliver us from evil. Amen.	8

Number 9

Do you know that you have a Guardian Angel?

God has nine different types of angels working for Him.

Seraphim	1
Cherubim	2
Thrones	3
Dominions	4
Powers	5
Virtues	6
Principalities	7
Archangels	8
Angels	9

Number 10

God the Father gave us 10 Commandments to help us to be holy like Him.

1   There is only one God, and we worship Him alone.

2   Keep God's name holy.

3   Keep Sunday holy.

4   Obey your father and mother.

5   Do not kill anyone.

6   A husband and wife must be faithful to each other.

7   Do not steal.

8   Do not lie.

9   Do not desire a person who is already married.

10   Do not desire what others have.

You *can* count to 10!
God bless you!

Scriptural References

All scriptural references are from *The Holy Bible: Douay-Rheims Version.*

Number 1	Ephesians 4:6
Number 2	Genesis 6:5 – 9:17
Number 3	Luke 1:26-38
Number 4	2 Peter 1:20-21
Number 5	John 20:19-31
Number 6	Genesis 1:1 – 2:3
Number 7	Isaiah 11:1-4

Number 8

Matthew 6:9-15
John 6:51-59
1 Corinthians 11:23-29

Number 9

Genesis 3:20-24
Isaiah 6:1-3
Matthew 18:10
Romans 8:33-39
Ephesians 1:17-23
Colossians 1:15-20
Jude 1:6-10

Number 10

Deuteronomy 5:1-22

1   I am the LORD your God: you shall not have strange gods before me.
2   You shall not take the name of the LORD your God in vain.
3   Remember to keep holy the LORD'S Day.
4   Honor your father and your mother.
5   You shall not kill.
6   You shall not commit adultery.
7   You shall not steal.
8   You shall not bear false witness against your neighbor.
9   You shall not covet your neighbor's wife.
10 You shall not covet your neighbor's goods.

Definitions

Counsel
The gift of the Holy Spirit that enables a person to judge promptly and rightly.

Fear of the Lord
The gift of the Holy Spirit that inspires a holy fear or profound respect for the majesty of God.

Fortitude
[fawr-ti-tood, -tyood] Also known as courage. The gift of the Holy Spirit that gives a person a special strength of will.

Gospels
The life and teachings of Jesus Christ as written in four books of the Bible according to Matthew, Mark, Luke, and John.

Hallowed
To make or recognize as sacred and to treat as holy.

Knowledge
The gift of the Holy Spirit that enables a person to "see" everything from a supernatural viewpoint.

Piety
[pahy-i-tee] The gift of the Holy Spirit that produces an instinctive love of God.

Trespasses
Sins or acts of injustice.

Understanding
The gift of the Holy Spirit that helps the mind grasp revealed truths.

Wisdom
The gift of the Holy Spirit that makes the soul responsive to God in the contemplation of all that is divine.

Made in the USA
Charleston, SC
18 December 2014